Mantras
of
The Mother

SRI AUROBINDO ASHRAM
PONDICHERRY

First published in three parts
in 1975, 1076 and 1977

First edition (combined) 1983
Seventh impression 2010

Rs 95
ISBN 978-81-7058-179-6

© Sri Aurobindo Ashram Trust 1983
Published by Sri Aurobindo Ashram Publication Department
Pondicherry 605 002
Web http://www.sabda.in

Printed at Sri Aurobindo Ashram Press, Pondicherry
PRINTED IN INDIA

Publisher's Note

The 274 sayings in this book, reproduced here in facsimile, were written by the Mother in 1954: For a period of nine months she wrote one saying a day in the diary of an Ashram sadhak. Most of these sayings are original sentences, written expressly for the sadhak. About one-third, however, are translations by the Mother of sentences first written earlier in her *Prières et Méditations*. These translations occur mainly in the diary entries for the last four months of the year. There are also a few sayings not by the Mother but by others; they were copied by her from *The Eternal Wisdom*, a collection of sayings of various thinkers and sages of the world. Seven entries here are known to be from that book: those of April 30, July 13 and September 19, 20, 21, 23 and 25.

How beautiful, grand, simple and calm everything becomes, when our thoughts turn to the Divine and we give ourselves to the Divine.

With my blessings.

The Mother

When you start a
quarrel it is as if
you were declaring
war to the Divine's
work.

With blessings

M.

*Whatever you do,
do it always carefully*

my blessings

For the work, steadiness
and regularity are as
necessary as skill.

with my blessings

My help is always
with you to help you
in your progress and
your work.

The difficulties you can
not overcome to-day,
will be over come to-morrow
or later on
with my blessings

Be sure that I am always present among you to guide and help you in your work and your sadhana with my blessings

One can progress through meditation, but through work provided it is done in the right spirit, one can progress ten times more.

With my blessings

Go on aspiring and
the necessary progress
is bound to come.

With my blessings

It is by combined
and patient effort
that all good work
is done.

With my blessings

Let it be, for you, a new birth of your consciousness, the constant and conscious contact with your psychic being, and, for your co-workers, the new start of an unselfish and real collaboration in the work.

With my blessings

Let the Consciousness
work in you and
through you and
everything will become
all right

with my blessings

Whenever things become difficult we must remain quiet and silent

with my blessings

Perfection in the work
must be the aim —,
but it is only by a
very patient effort that
this can be obtained

my blessings

on a previous page
the prayer was
" quiet all violence,
let Thy love reign. "
with my blessings

Life is a journey in the darkness of the night - Wake up to the inner light.

with my blessings

M.

Daily we must aspire
to conquer all mistakes,
all obscurities, all
ignorances –

With my blessings

A great joy is always
deep in our heart,
and always we can
find it there —

with my blessings

It is in the Divine
that we shall always
find all what we
need . blessings

Alone the Divine can give us a perfect safety.

with my blessings

whenever there is
sincerity and good will
the Divine's help also
is there

with my blessings

With trust in the
Divine's Grace all
obstacles can be
surmounted

with my blessings

At the hour of
danger a perfect
quietness is required

with my blessings

Let the Divine Consciousness
be the leading power in
your life.

With my blessings

The best way to express
one's gratitude to the
Divine is to feel
simply happy.

with my blessings

We celebrated on this date the 34½ anniversary of my final arrival at Pondicherry – Since then I have not left this place.

My blessings

Steady efforts always bring great results

with my blessings

There is no end to progress and every day one can learn to do better what one does

with my blessings

Let the Divine Presence
be always with you.
my blessings

Take Truth for your force,
Take Truth for your refuge.

With my blessings

We must always aspire
to be free from all
ignorance and to
have a true faith.

With my blessings

An old wisdom says:
"Just as unity is in each
of the numbers, so the Divine
is one in all things."
With my blessings

There is no greater courage
than that of recognising
one's own mistakes

with my blessings

always do what you
know to be the best
even if it is the most
difficult thing to do.

with my blessings

There is no greater
victory than that
of controling oneself

with my blessings

The true strength
is always peaceful.

my blessings

Whatever you do,
always remember the
Divine.

With my blessings

Everything must be
transformed by the
knowledge of the Truth.

With my blessings

In the Divine's love
we always find all
suport and all
consolation

with blessings

M.

Let the Divine's peace
always reign in your
heart and mind.
with my blessings

The only important
thing is to follow the
Divine's truth with
love and joy.

My blessings

The Grace will never fail us - such is the faith we must keep constantly in our heart.

With my blessings

How beautiful, grand,
simple and calm
everything becomes, when
our thoughts turn to
the Divine and we
give ourselves to the
Divine!

with my blessings

In peace and silence
the Eternal manifest.
Let nothing trouble
you and the Eternal
will manifest
With my blessings

If man surrenders
totally to the Divine,
he identifies himself
with the Divine.

My blessings

There is no greater joy than to serve the Divine.

With my blessings

When we trust in
the Divine's Grace we
get an unfailing courage.

With my blessings

With a quiet mind
and a peaceful heart,
let us do the work
happily.

With my blessings

The truth is in us,
we have only to
become aware of it.

with my blessings

M.

After all, it is very simple, we have only to become what we are in the depths of our being.

with my blessings

Let us have a sincere
aspiration united to a
constant good-will
and the victory is
certain.

With my blessings

J.

Let us do our best in all circumstances, leaving the result to the Divine's decision,

with my blessings

A constant aspiration
conquers all defects.

with my blessings

The Divine is present
in the very atoms
of our body.

with my blessings

Day after day our
aspiration will grow
and our faith will
intensify.

with my blessings

Let us always do
the right thing and
we shall always
be quiet and happy.

with my blessings

We must never forget
that our goal is to
manifest the Supramental
Reality

with my blessings

We must be free of
all selfishness to serve
properly the Divine's cause

with my blessings

In the silence of
our heart there
is always peace
and joy.

With my blessings
M.

The storm is only at the surface of the sea; in the depths all is quiet.

With my blessings

The physical being itself
can be the seat of
perfect existence, knowledge
and bliss.

With my blessings

In full appreciation
of the way in which
the work is proceeding —
With my blessings

My blessings at the
beginning of the
third month of
your good work.

M.—

Do not think of what
you have been, think
only of what you want
to be and you are
sure to progress.

With my blessings

Do not look behind,
look always in front,
at what you want
to do — and you are
sure of progressing

with my blessings

Every day, at each moment, my blessings are with you.

Have full trust in
the Divine's Grace and
the Divine's Grace will
help you in all ways.

With my blessings

Let us seek our
happiness only in
the Divine

with my blessings

Keep yourself free
from all human
attachment and
you will be happy
with my blessings

With the Divine's help
nothing is impossible.

My blessings

If earnestly you say
to the Divine: " I want
only Thee", the Divine
will arrange the circumstances
in such a way that
you are compelled
to be sincere.

with my blessings

M.

Soar very high
and you will discover
the great depths.

with my blessings

The Divine manifests
upon earth whenever
and wherever it is
possible.

with my blessings

Open yourself more
and more to the
Divine's force and
your work will progress
steadily towards perfection

With my blessings

The Force is there waiting
to be manifested, we
must discover the new
forms through which
it can manifest.

    with my blessings

It is in an unshakeable
peace that can be found
the true power.

With my blessings

A quiet endurance
is the sure way to
success.

With my blessings

A simple and
faithful heart is
a great boon.

With my blessings

In each heart, the Divine's
Presence is the promise
of future and possible
perfections   with my blessings

Only those who are
already very sincere
know that they are
not completely sincere

With my blessings

In a quiet silence
strength is restored

With my blessings

When waking up every morning, let us pray for a day of complete consecration.

With my blessings

Before going to sleep every night, we must pray that the mistakes we may have committed during the day should not be repeated in future.

With my blessings

Let us keep flaming
in our heart the
fire of progress.

With my blessings.

Every day, at each moment, we shall aspire to do the right thing in the right way, always.

With my blessings

For the body, to know means to be able to do. In fact the body knows only what it can do.

With my blessings

All veils must be
dissolved and the
light must shine
fully in the hearts
of all —

with my blessings

What cannot be done to-day will surely be done later on. No effort for progress has ever been made in vain.

With my blessings

New forms are needed
for the manifestation
of a new Force.
with my blessings

We must be satisfied
with what the Divine gives
us, and do what He
wants us to do without
weakness, free from
useless ambition.

With my blessings

All sincere prayers
are granted, but it
may take some time
to realise materially.

with my blessings

The more we know
the more we can see
that we do not know

with my blessings

It is easier to suppress
than to organise, but
the true order is far
superior to suppression.

With my blessings

Our mind must be
silent and quiet
but our heart must
be full of an ardent
aspiration.

With my blessings

We must replace competition and strife by collaboration and fraternity.

With my blessings

Let each suffering
pave the way to
transformation.

With my blessings

No joy is comparable
to the feeling of the
eternal Presence in
one's heart.

With my blessings

It is only in the
Divine that we can
find perfect peace
and total satisfaction
with my blessings

We must march on
with the quiet certitude
that what has to be
done will be done.

With my blessings

The supramental force is
ready for manifestation,
let us get ready also
and it will manifest.

With my blessings

When the Supramental
manifests, an unequalled
joy spreads over the earth.

With my blessings

Drop all fear, all strife, all quarrels, open your eyes and your hearts — the Supramental force is there —

With my blessings

M.

With patience, strength, courage and a calm and indomitable energy we shall prepare ourselves to receive the Supramental Force.

With my blessings

The mind must remain
quiet to let the Force
flow through it for
an integral manifestation.

With my blessings

The chief purpose of
the "avatar" is to give
to men a concrete proof
that the Divine can
manifest upon earth

with my blessings

Contemplate the mirror
of your heart and you
shall taste little by little
a pure joy and an
unmixed peace.

With my blessings

Look into the depths
of your heart and you
will see there the
Divine Presence

With my blessings

When the aspiration is
awake each day brings
us nearer to the goal.

With my blessings

Not only the mind
and the vital, but
the body also in all
its cells must aspire
for the divine transformation.

With my blessings

Each one is responsible
only of the sincerity
of his aspiration

With my blessings

With our own perfection
grows in us a generous
understanding of the
others

with my blessings

It is difficult to get rid of all habits They must be faced with a steady determination.

With my blessings

When you reach the contact with the Divine's love you see this love in everything and all circumstances ... with my blessings

All sincere prayers
are granted, every call
is answered.

With my blessings

Before getting angry
for the mistakes of others
one should always remember
one's own mistakes.
   With my blessings

Let us progress ourselves,
it is the best way of
making the others progress.

With my blessings

The Divine's love and knowledge must always govern our thoughts and actions.

With my blessings

We ought to be in a
constant state of aspiration,
but when we cannot aspire
let us pray with the
simplicity of a child.

With my blessings

Satisfaction does not depend
on outer circumstances
but on an inner
condition.

With my blessings

We are upon earth
to manifest the
Divine's will

With my blessings

It is always a mistake
to complain about the
circumstances of our life,
for they are the outward
expression of what we
are ourselves.

with my blessings

We must decide to get rid of all doubts, they are among the worst enemies of our progress.

with my blessings

It is our lack of faith
that creates our limitations

with my blessings

There is no greater courage
than to be always truthful.
with my blessings

New words are needed
to express new ideas,
new forms are necessary
to manifest new forces.

With my blessings

Our courage and
   endurance must be
as great as our hope
and our hope has
no limits.
   with my blessings

In the Divine Consciousness
the smallest things from
below unite with
the highest, the most
sublime from above

With my blessings

It is ages of ardent
aspiration that have
brought us here to
do the Divine's Work.

With my blessings

Whenever there is any
difficulty we must always
remember that we are
here exclusively to accomplish
the Divine's will.

With my blessings

And when our adhesion
to the Divine's will is
total then also our
peace and joy become
total

with my blessings

Behind the surface of things there is a sea of perfect consciousness in which we can always dip.

With my blessings

yy. —

Whatever is the difficulty
if we keep truly quiet
the solution will come
with my blessings

This earth is still governed by ignorance and falsehood. But the time has come for the manifestation of Truth.

with my blessings

All mischief comes
from a lack of balance.

So, let us keep our balance
carefully, always, in
all circumstances.

with my blessings

M.

The Divine Consciousness
must be our only
guide.

With my blessings

The Divine Consciousness
is the only true help,
the only true happiness.
With my blessings

We must never forget
that we are here
to serve the Supramental
Truth and Light and
to prepare its manifestation
in ourselves and upon
the earth.

    with my blessings

Sri Aurobindo is always with us, enlightening, guiding, protecting.

We must answer to his grace by a perfect faithfulness.

With my blessings

A steady hope helps
much on the way.
with my blessings

Faith is the surest guide in the darkest days.

with my blessings

The Divine Grace is with us and never leaves us even when the appearances are dark.

With my blessings

In each human being
there is a beast crouching
ready to manifest at the
slightest unwatchfulness.
The only remedy is a
constant vigilance.

With my blessings

When the path is known
it is easy to tread upon
it.

With my blessings

The things we cannot
realise to-day we shall
be able to realise to-morrow.
The only necessity is to
endure—

With my blessings

Each new progress in the universal expression means the possibility of a new manifestation.

with my blessings

Our hopes are never
too great for manifestation
We cannot conceive of
anything that can not
be -

with blessings

The Supreme's power
is infinite — it is
our faith that is small

with my blessings

The offering of our being
we make to the Divine
must be integral and
effective.

with my blessings

M.

Our thoughts are still
ignorant, they must be
enlightened.
Our aspiration is still
imperfect, it must be
purified.
Our action is still powerless,
it must become effective.

with my blessings

So much obscurity
has fallen upon earth
that only the supramental
manifestation can
dissolve it.

with my blessings

Let us constantly aspire
to be a perfect instrument
for the Divine's work.

With my blessings

Blessed will be the day
when the earth, awaken
to the Truth, ~~will~~ lives
only for the Divine

with my blessings

The Truth is in you —
but you must want it,
in order to realise it.
With my blessings

Man is the intermediary being between what is and what is to be realised.

With my blessings

Let us advance always,
without stopping, towards
an always more complete
manisfestation, an always
more complete and higher
consciousness

with my blessings

My blessings
are always
with you

In an unshakeable
faith lies all our
hope.

with my blessings

To follow the path
to the end, one
must be armed
with a very patient
endurance.

With my blessings

On the spiritual
path each step forward
is a conquest and
the result of a fight.

With my blessings

The victory is to
the most enduring.

With my blessings

The victory of yesterday must be only one step towards to-morrow's victory.

With my blessings

Outside the Divine all is
falsehood and illusion,
all is mournful obscurity.

My blessings

The Lord has said,
"The time is come"
and all the obstacles
will be overcome

My blessings

The Divine is the saviour of all life and the reason of all activity, the goal of our thoughts

with my blessings

The Divine's Peace must dwell constantly in our hearts.

with my blessings

The Divine's Presence
is for us an absolute,
immutable, invariable
fact.

With my blessings

In peace and silence
the Eternal manifests;
allow nothing to disturb
you and the Eternal
will manifest.

With my blessings

In the Divine, by the Divine, all is transfigured and glorified; in the Divine is found the key of all mysteries and all powers

With my blessings

The power of the human intelligence is without bounds, it increases by concentration, that is the secret.

With my blessings

How many efforts and
struggles again to give
ourselves, to surrender, once
the individuality is
constituted!

with my blessings

We must watch over our thoughts - A bad thought is the most dangerous of thieves.

With my blessings

It is the Lord who sets all in motion from the depths of the being; it is His will that directs, His force that acts.

With my blessings

Often man is preoccupied
with human rules and
forgets the inner law.

With my blessings

Let not the talk
of the vulgar make
any impression on
you.

my blessings

The sage is never alone ...
he bears in himself the
Lord of all things

In all there lacks the unchanging peace of the Divine's sovereign contemplation, and the calm vision of the Divine's immutable eternity.

With my blessings

The mind is a clear and
polished mirror and
our continual duty is to
keep it pure and never
allow dust to accumulate
upon it.

With my blessings

A new light shall
break upon the earth,
a new world shall
be born, and the things
that were announced
shall be fulfilled.
With my blessings

Do not believe all that men say, but blush not to submit to a sage who knows more than thyself.

With my blessings

It is in the most complete
peace, serenity and equality
that all is the Divine
even as the Divine is all

With my blessings

Like the child who does
not reason and has no
care trust thyself to
the Divine that His
will may be done

My blessings

The joy of perfect
union can come only
when what has to be
done is done

with my blessings

O, to see no longer the appearances which change incessantly; to contemplate only The Divine's immutable oneness in everything and every where !

With my blessings

We aspire to be the valiant warriors of the Lord so that His glory may manifest upon the earth.

With my blessings

In the Divine's light we shall see, in the Divine's knowledge we shall know, in the Divine's will we shall realise...

With my blessings

Outside the Divine all
is falsehood and illusion,
all is mournful obscurity.
In the Divine is life, light
and joy. In the Divine is
the sovereign Peace.

With my blessings

In the sincerity
of our trust lies
the certitude of
our victory.

    With my blessings

. All our strength
is with the Divine
with Him we can
surmount all
the obstacles

with my blessings

When the Divine grants
the true inner happiness
nothing in the world
has the power to snatch
it away.

With my blessings

It is Victory Day; let
it be a true victory
of the Spirit over ignorance
and falsehood.

With my blessings

The Divine's voice is heard
as a melodious chant
in the stillness of the heart.

with my blessings

At each moment of our life, in all circumstances the Grace is there helping us to surmount all difficulties.

With my blessings

The Divine's triumph is so perfect that every obstacle, every ill-will, every hatred rising against Him is a promise of a vaster and still completer victory.

with my blessings

The resistance with
which we meet in the
accomplishment of
our work is proportionate
to its importance

with my blessings

The supramental force
has the power to transform
even the darkest hate
in luminous peace.

With my blessings

Every obstacle must disappear, in every part of the being, the darkness of the ignorance must be replaced by the Divine's knowledge

With my blessings

often we cling to that which
was, afraid of losing the result
of a precious experience, of
giving up a vast and high
consciousness and falling
again into an inferior
state. But we must
always look forward
and advance.

with my blessings

What can he fear, he who belongs to the Divine? Can he not walk, his soul expanding and his brow illumined, upon the path the Divine traces for him whatever it may be, even if it is altogether incomprehensible to his limited reason?

With my blessings

Let us adore in silence
and listen to the Divine
in a deep concentration.
With my blessings.

The Divine's will is that
we should be like channels
always open, always
more wide, so that His
forces may pour their
abundance into the
world.

With my blessings

Our will must always be a perfect expression of the Divine's Will

With my blessings

The night also is full of promises and we must face it with full faith and confidence.

With my blessings

There is no greater
bliss than that of being
like a new-born child
in front of the Divine.

With my blessings

The immutable Beatitude of
the Divine is translated in
the consciousness by an
impelling force of progress
of an incomparable
intensity

With my blessings

This force is transformed in the most external being into a calm and assured will which no obstacle can overthrow

With my blessings

The Divine's Will is that
the mind should know and
He says "Awake and be
conscious of the Truth".

with my blessings

We aspire to be liberated
from all ignorance,
liberated from our ego
so that we may open
wide the doors of the
Supramental's glorious
manifestation.

With my blessings

All our life, all our work must be a constant aspiration towards the supramental perfection

With my blessings

Whatever happens
we must remain quiet
and trust ✦ the
Divine's Grace

with my blessings

Remaining steady in our effort and quiet and firm in our determination, we are sure to reach the goal.

with my blessings

In the perfect silence
of the contemplation all
widens to infinity, and
in the perfect peace of
that silence the Divine
appears in the resplendent
glory of His light

with my blessings

Our constant prayer
is to understand the
Divine's will and to
live accordingly.

With my blessings

May the Divine's love dwell
as the sovereign Master
of our hearts and the
Divine's knowledge never
leave our thoughts.
With my blessings

Appearances and rules change, but our faith and our aim remain the same —

With My blessings

We must be always,
solely and exclusively,
the servitors of the
Divine.

With my blessings

Our aspiration rises
always identical, supported
by a concentrated will.
With my blessings

We pray that the Divine
should teach us ever more,
enlighten us more and more,
dispel our ignorance,
illumine our minds.

With my blessings

At every moment all the unforeseen, the unexpected, the unknown is before us — and what happens to us depends mostly on the intensity and purity of our faith.

With my blessings

At every minute the
universe is recreated in
its totality and in each
of its parts.

With my blessings

If we had a truly living faith, an absolute certitude of the almighty power of the Divine, His manifestation could be so evident that the whole earth would be transformed by it.

With my blessings

All is mute in the being,
but in the bosom of the
silence burns the lamp
that can never be
extinguished, the fire
of an ardent aspiration
to know and to live
integrally the Divine.

With my blessings

The flame of the aspiration must be so straight and so ardent that no obstacle can dissolve it.

With my blessings

In concentration and
silence we must
gather strength for the
right action.

With my blessings

We must gather
ourselves in a calm
resolution and an
unshakeable resolute.
With my blessings

For the plenitude of His light we invoke the Divine, to awaken is us the power to express Him.

With my blessings

The serene and immobile
Consciousness watches at
the bounderies of the world
as a Sphinx of eternity.
And yet to some it gives
out its secret.

with my blessings

We have, therefore, the certitude that what has to be done will be done, and that our present individual being is really called upon to collaborate in this glorious victory, in this new manifestation.

with my blessings

None can say to the Divine; "I have known Thee", and yet all carry Him in themselves, and in the silence of their soul can hear the echo of the Divine's voice.

With my blessings

Upon this world of illusion
this sombre nightmare, the
Divine has bestowed His
sublime Reality, and each
atom of matter contains
something of His Eternity

with my blessings

The only important thing
is the goal to be attained.
The way matters little, and
often it is better not to
know it in advance.

With my blessings

It is in oneself that there
are all the obstacles, it
is in oneself that there
are all the difficulties,
it is in oneself that there
are all the darkness and
all the ignorance

With my blessings

There is a great
power in the simple
confidence of a
child

With my blessings

The Divine's words comfort and bliss, soothe and illumine and the Divine's generous hand lifts a fold of the veil which hides the infinite knowledge.

With my blessings

How calm, noble and
pure is the splendour
of the Divine's Contemplation.

With my blessings

We must be before the Divine always like a page perfectly blank, so that the Divine Will may be inscribed in us without any difficulty or mixture.

With my blessings

The very memory of the past experience has sometimes to be swept away from the thoughts that it may not impede the work of perpetual reconstruction, which, alone in this world of relativities, permits the perfect manifestation of the Divine.

With my blessings

At each moment may
our attitude be such that
the Divine's Will determines
our choice. ~~and~~ so that
the Divine may give the
direction to all our life.

With my blessings

To live in the Divine with
a life quite new, a life
solely made of the Divine,
of which the Divine should
be the sovereign Lord ...
and so all troubles will
be transformed into
serenity, all anguish
into peace.

With my blessings

We feel the Divine so living
in us that we await events
with serenity, knowing that
His way is everywhere since
we carry it in our being

with blessings

We must be freed from
all care for contingences;
we must be delivered
from the ordinary outlook
on things

with my blessings

We must see - only through
the Divine's eyes and
act only through the
Divine's will.

With my blessings

The Divine's love can generate in all peace and the satisfaction that comes from benevolence.

With my blessings

Our heart is purified from
trouble and anguish; it
is firm and calm, and
feels the Divine in everything.

With my blessings

The individual existence is a canticle perpetually renewed, that the universe offers to the inconceivable splendour of the Divine

with my blessings

It is only the Divine's
Grace that can give
peace, happiness, power, light,
knowledge, beatitude and
love in their essence
and their truth.

with my blessings

In failure as well
as in success, the
Divine's Grace is
always there.

With my blessings

in the integrality and
absoluteness of bhakti
and surrender, we find
the essential condition
of perfect peace leading
to uninterrupted bliss

With my blessings

In a total surrender to the
Divine there can be no longer
errors or faults or any
insufficiency since it is
what the Divine has willed
that He does and it is
done as the Divine has
willed it.

with my blessings

There is a thirst for Love
which no human relation
can quench. It is only
the Divine's love that
can satisfy that thirst.
with my blessings

It is with the confidence of a child that our heart implores the Divine.

With my blessings

The day comes when all barriers have fallen, no thens and arround us and we can feel like the bird that opens its wings for an unopposed soar

with my blessings

Whatever we do, we must always remember our aim.

with blessings

The errors can become
stepping-stones, the blind
gropings can be changed
in conquests.

With my blessings

The Divine's glory transforms
defeats into eternity's victories;
all shadows have fled before
His radiant brightness.
With my blessings

Truth is eternally beyond
all that we can think
or say of it.

With my blessings

At certain periods, the whole terrestrial life seems to pass miraculously through stages which, at other times, it would take thousands of years to traverse,

with my blessings

at every moment one
must know how to
lose everything in order
to gain everything, to
shed the past as a dead
body and be reborn into
a greater plenitude

with my blessings

The Divine's Presence gives
us peace in strength, serenity
in action and an unchanging
happiness in the midst of
all circumstances.

With my blessings

All barriers must be
thrown down one after
the other, for the being to
put on the integral
amplitude of all the
possibilities of manifestation

With my blessings

One can live the Divine
even though unable to
express the Divine, one
can realise and be the
Divine's infinity though
unable to define or
explain the Divine.

With my blessings

Always the Supreme will remain the eternal mystery calling for all our wonder and marvelling.

With my blessings

For him who is in union
with the Divine, everywhere
is the Divine's perfect felicity,
in every place and in every
circumstance it is with
him

With my blessings

Like the child who does not reason and has no care we trust ourselves to the Divine that the Divine's Will may be done.

With my blessings

It is never in vain
that an ardent and
sincere prayer is
addressed to the
Divine's Grace.

With blessings

The Supreme is divine
Knowledge and perfect Unity;
at each moment of the
day let us call to Him
so that we may be nothing
else than Himself.

With my blessings

When, in our despair, we
cry to the Divine, always
He answers to our call

With my blessings

The Divine is the unalloyed happiness, the blissful felicity, but this felicity is perfect only when it is integral

With my blessings

The Divine is the sure
friend who never fails,
the Power, the Support, the Guide.
The Divine is the Light which
scatters darkness, the Conqueror
who assures the victory.

With my blessings

A new light shall
break upon the earth,
a light of Truth and
Harmony.

With my blessings

At the service of the Divine
we are; it is the Divine
who decides, ordains and
puts in motion, directs
and accomplishes the
action.

With my blessings

The soul cannot think the Divine but knows Him with certitude.

With my blessings

We pray the Divine to
accept the ardent flame
of our gratitude and
of our joyous and fully
confident adherence.

With my blessings

We must know how to give
our life and also our death,
our happiness and also our
suffering.

with my blessings

We must know how to depend for everything and in everything on the Divine — He alone can surmount all difficulties.

With my blessings

In this last day of
the year, let us take
the resolution that all
our weaknesses and
obstinate obscurities will
drop from us along
with the finishing year.
With my blessings

good bye to the
previous year –
Welcome to the
new one –

blessings